Coaching for Results

A Skills-Based Workshop

Participant Workbook

Donna Berry, Charles Cadwell, and Joe Fehrmann

Human Resource Development Press, Inc.
Amherst, Massachusetts

Published by HRD Press
22 Amherst Road
Amherst, MA 01002
1-800-822-2801

ISBN 0-87425-318-7

Production services by Clark Riley

Cover design by Art Torres

Editorial services by Robie Grant

Contents

Introduction

Teams. Coaches. "Win one for the Gipper." You have probably heard all the athletic analogies that have become an accepted part of today's business lexicon. Yet there is little doubt that today's managers and supervisors are expected to have the ability to lead and coach their employees.

Coaching is not just telling people what to do; it also involves helping them achieve their fullest potential. Successful coaches have to assume a variety of other roles such as team leader, counselor, listener, facilitator, and director. At the same time they are expected to push decision making down the line in order to empower their people.

This *Coaching for Results* Workshop is designed to help you develop the skills necessary to be a successful coach and to prepare a plan to put those skills into practice.

In order to get the most out of the training, you'll be expected to participate in a variety of ways, including:

- role plays
- group discussion
- small group activities
- case studies

This *Workbook* will be your primary resource during the training. During each session you will use the *Workbook* to take notes, complete individual exercises, and to participate in small group discussions.

After training, your notes will turn the *Workbook* into your own personalized reference manual that you can use back on the job. It will contain the action ideas that you want to implement with your work group.

The *Workbook* also includes several job aids that provide additional information that may not be covered in detail during the training. These are key points that will supplement the classroom activities and that you'll want to refer to as you develop your coaching skills.

Remember, this is a workbook—not a study book that you read and then set on a shelf. Bring your *Workbook* with you to every training session and use it as you "work" through the training. After the training, your completed *Workbook* will be something that you'll refer to often in the future.

Role of the Coach

The best coaches set in motion a continuing learning process—that, we find, helps people develop a tolerance for their own struggles and accelerates the unfolding of skill and contributions that would not have been possible without the "magic" attention of a dedicated coach.

Nancy Austen and Tom Peters
A Passion for Excellence

The Role of Coach

In order to achieve as an effective coach, it is important for each of us to be able to describe and define what the term "coach" conjures in our mind. Whether or not we have ever taken an active part in athletics, each of us has benefited from the influence of some person in our lives who displayed essential coaching qualities.

As you work through this section of your learning experience, we ask that you think back to a person or persons who taught, guided, and challenged you. If they meet the accepted definition of coach, as it relates to the workplace, they also encouraged, supported, and sometimes offered corrective solutions to problems you encountered.

With the image of that person in your mind, it will be easier to list important personal and professional characteristics. It is often said that effective coaches communicate well—honestly, openly—and that they listen even better. They are counted among the tutors of our lives, and they never hesitated to provide remedial instruction when they saw insufficiency. They were often our most enthusiastic cheerleaders, a highly appropriate term for the coaches of America's work force.

You will be asked to rate the benefits of the coaching approach. There are many. You will be asked to think about your own skill levels as they impact this important role. And you will become excited with the anticipation of employees who display greater self-esteem, exhibit higher morale, produce at a greater level, and enjoy more job satisfaction.

The term was taken from athletics and for good reason. We coaches of the workplace must achieve with a diverse group of people, all with different skills or skill levels, toward a mutual objective to produce a "winning" product or service. In a time when the competition is keen, and resources are limited, coaching appears to be one of the better ideas embraced by American business.

Coaches Hall of Fame

Coaches Famous to Me

1. Who provided an "aha" experience for you that allowed you to see meaning in an event or experience or potential within yourself?

   _____

   _____

   _____

   _____

2. Who provided you with a quote that has had great meaning for you? Perhaps you have repeated it or it has influenced your thinking or actions. Write the quote and where it came from.

   _____

   _____

   _____

   _____

3. Who helped you to uncover, develop, or use a talent, ability, or interest that had lain dormant? Name that person, your skill, and the incident.

   _____

   _____

   _____

   _____

   _____

   _____

Adapted and printed with permission from *Mentoring, A Practical Guide*.
Gordon F. Shea, Crisp Publications, Los Altos, CA, 1992.

Coaching Defined and Described

Coaching *defined* ...

Coaching *described ..., characteristics include:*

- ➲ _____
- ➲ _____
- ➲ _____
- ➲ _____
- ➲ _____
- ➲ _____
- ➲ _____
- ➲ _____
- ➲ _____
- ➲ _____
- ➲ _____
- ➲ _____

Coaching Benefits Rating Form

Use this form to assess your current work situation. Are the benefits of effective coaching obvious? To what degree? A great deal? Little or no evidence? Add any benefits that are apparent in your workplace but are not listed here.

Benefit	Little or No ↔ A Great Deal
1. Higher competency levels	1 2 3 4 5 6 7
2. Increased team attitude	1 2 3 4 5 6 7
3. Completion of quality work	1 2 3 4 5 6 7
4. Greater levels of creativity	1 2 3 4 5 6 7
5. Personal accountability for work	1 2 3 4 5 6 7
6. Acceptance of new challenges	1 2 3 4 5 6 7
7. Cooperation, collaboration	1 2 3 4 5 6 7
8. More and better listening	1 2 3 4 5 6 7
9. More people development	1 2 3 4 5 6 7
10. Increased productivity	1 2 3 4 5 6 7
11. Positive feedback and reward	1 2 3 4 5 6 7
12. Willingness to delegate	1 2 3 4 5 6 7
13. Greater empowerment	1 2 3 4 5 6 7
14.	1 2 3 4 5 6 7
15.	1 2 3 4 5 6 7
16.	1 2 3 4 5 6 7

Scoring consistently in the 5-7 range indicates an effective coaching environment. Scoring more often in the 1-3 range signals a need for more practiced coaching skills.

Coaching Benefits Rating Form

Use this form to assess your current work situation. Are the benefits of effective coaching obvious? To what degree? A great deal? Little or no evidence? Add any benefits that are apparent in your workplace but are not listed here.

Benefit	Little or No ↔ A Great Deal
1. Higher competency levels	1 2 3 4 5 6 7
2. Increased team attitude	1 2 3 4 5 6 7
3. Completion of quality work	1 2 3 4 5 6 7
4. Greater levels of creativity	1 2 3 4 5 6 7
5. Personal accountability for work	1 2 3 4 5 6 7
6. Acceptance of new challenges	1 2 3 4 5 6 7
7. Cooperation, collaboration	1 2 3 4 5 6 7
8. More and better listening	1 2 3 4 5 6 7
9. More people development	1 2 3 4 5 6 7
10. Increased productivity	1 2 3 4 5 6 7
11. Positive feedback and reward	1 2 3 4 5 6 7
12. Willingness to delegate	1 2 3 4 5 6 7
13. Greater empowerment	1 2 3 4 5 6 7
14.	1 2 3 4 5 6 7
15.	1 2 3 4 5 6 7
16.	1 2 3 4 5 6 7

Scoring consistently in the 5-7 range indicates an effective coaching environment.
Scoring more often in the 1-3 range signals a need for more practiced coaching skills.

Communication

What you do speaks so loud that I cannot hear what you say.

Ralph Waldo Emerson

Communication

Nearly every survey of an organization's climate, management practices, or culture will have one thing in common. When one member of the organization is asked to identify what needs improvement, the number one area of concern is "communication." Communication is vital to every aspect of our lives and, for better or for worse, it is going on all the time. Our personal lives, our professional relationships, our teams, our careers, all revolve around how effectively we communicate.

Communication is a rather simple process, really. In its most basic form, it consists of a sender, a message, and a receiver. Additionally, filters—"obstacles," perceptions, vocabulary, biases, physical characteristics—alter the message as it is sent and as it is received. All of these elements combined comprise what is known as the "feedback loop."

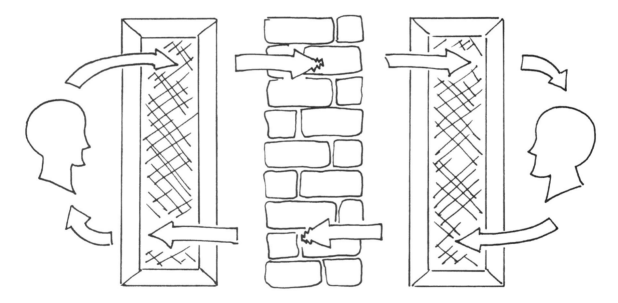

Obviously, a lot can go wrong with this communication process, which is not nearly so simple as it looks or as many people believe. Both the sender's and the receiver's filters affect the message. Their education, training, and cultural backgrounds can cause words and gestures to have vastly different meanings. Physical distance or status in an organization are typical "obstacles" that tend to slow or stop the message. And the feedback loop contains all these features as well!

Both the sender and the receiver must work hard to overcome the problems caused by filters and obstacles. They should…

Senders
- Send clear, understandable messages.
- Use language and terms the receiver understands.
- Be sensitive to clues that reveal how the receiver is "getting" the message.
- Make sure their verbal message and nonverbal signals (such as gestures or facial expressions) support each other.

Receivers
- From time to time, check to be sure they understand the message.
- Show they are paying attention with eye contact, nods, and other listening responses.
- Be courteous in their reactions— by avoiding interrupting or reacting negatively during the message.

Communication, then, is an ability that requires many skills. For a coach or mentor, the most critical one is listening. Effective coaches and mentors understand how important it is to show they are listening, to check to be sure they have understood, and to demonstrate their acceptance of how others feel.

Listening Errors

• Inattention

_____

_____

_____

_____

• Early Evaluation

_____

_____

_____

_____

• Judging Values

_____

_____

_____

_____

• Aggressive Behavior

_____

_____

_____

_____

• Debating

_____

_____

_____

_____

Keys to Effective Listening

KEY ONE: *ATTENTION*

_____

_____

_____

_____

KEY TWO: *UNDERSTANDING*

_____

_____

_____

Open-Ended Questions

Instructions: Write an open-ended question that will encourage the protégé (a person whose career is developed or promoted by you, the mentor, a person of influence) to discuss each of the topics listed below.

	Topic	**Open-Ended Question**
1.	You want to know what your protégé's career desires are.	_____ _____ _____
2.	You want to know whether your protégé liked his/her last boss.	_____ _____ _____
3.	You want to know whether your protégé likes his/her present assignment.	_____ _____ _____

Paraphrasing

Instructions: One of the skills in effective listening is the ability to paraphrase; that is, to repeat in one's own words what someone else said. Paraphrasing is harder than it might seem at first. Try it by having another person read one of the following statements to you. Then, you paraphrase what was said. Be careful—you should capture all of the speaker's ideas without adding or implying any opinions, values, or ideas of your own.

Statement A

I think what we're doing to our planet is nothing short of criminal. In fact, I think it's something like murder. The earth is all we've got, but here we are polluting the rivers, polluting the oceans, destroying the rain forest, extinguishing whole species of plants and animals. I think we ought to put a special tax on using water. Even well water, and especially water from rivers. We should limit lumber production to 25 percent of what it is now and require new homes to be made of 50 percent synthetic materials. We should require only paper sacks in grocery stores, because they can be recycled. We've got to stop kidding around and take this problem seriously.

Statement B

I'd like you to think about looking at your political affiliation in a new light, and change your party. I don't know if you're a Democrat or a Republican right now, but if you'd take the time to read the Constitution, I think you'd be surprised at how utterly wrong both parties are. I mean really *read* it; don't just skim it. You'd find out that the government has no Constitutional right to be doing 99 percent of the wasteful stuff it's doing. There's no allowance in the Constitution for the government to build roads, get involved in education, impose income tax, support the arts—isn't that NEA something else?—or build bridges, much less legislate our morality. Think about it. If you do, you'll change your mind.

Observer Feedback

Instructions: This conversation exercise includes three roles: the *Observer*, who will complete this form; the *Listener/Coach*, who will listen and respond in the conversation; and the *Speaker/Protégé*, who will begin the conversation. The *Speaker/Protégé* will select the topic of the conversation from the following list:

> My career plans
> My family plans
> My educational plans
> My retirement plans

If you are the *Speaker/Protégé*, take a few moments to gather your thoughts on the topic you choose. If you are the *Listener/Coach*, your role is to practice skills in Attention and Understanding. Keep the *Speaker/Protégé* actively involved and learn as much as you can about him or her. If you are the *Observer*, your role is to take note of all the ways the *Listener/Coach* practices the skills listed on this feedback worksheet. Use actual examples as much as you can.

NOTES

Key One: *Attention*　　　　　　_____

   Posture　　　　　　　　_____

   Facial Expression　　　　_____

   Eyes　　　　　　　　　_____

   Sounds　　　　　　　　_____

Key Two: *Understanding*　　_____

   Paraphrasing　　　　　　_____

   Reflecting　　　　　　　_____

   Questions　　　　　　　_____

   Acknowledging Emotion　_____

_____

To see how many people can be frustrated by our technical jargon, try "translating" these two statements. (*Hint:* They are both common phrases.)

1. Accelerated execution produces faulty results.

2. A superfluity of culinary experts disarrays the preparation of the fluid meat extract.

Answers:
2. Too many cooks spoils the broth.
1. Haste makes waste.

Some Tips to Improve Nonverbal Communicatio n

- Maintain friendly, steady eye contact. Be careful, though, not to stare or glare.
- Show you are listening through an attentive posture.
- Avoid showing disagreement or disapproval through facial expressions.
- Be sensitive to others' need for physical distance. Don't invade their "space" by being too close to them physically.

The Confrontational Situation:
Responding Rather Than Reacting

Six Steps for Dealing with Conflict

Few of us enjoy confrontational situations. Most people prefer to avoid them or smooth things over rather than deal with the underlying issues. Some of us will instinctively respond to confrontation by making demands, even yelling. While these natural reactions may be appropriate in a few circumstances; following the six steps listed below will yield a more thoughtful and productive response.

1. **Assess what is happening.**
   Be aware of the circumstances, collect data quickly. Remember that the self-esteem of the persons involved is in jeopardy.

2. **Accept your influence.**
   Stop wishing the person(s) were different; a great waste of time. Recognize your own ability to bring about a successful resolution.

3. **Take control of yourself.**
   If necessary, get some mental distance in order to control your emotions. Be aware of your personal hot-buttons and don't allow yourself to lose objectivity.

4. **Formulate a plan of appropriate response.**
   Resist your instinctive reactions; they may not be right for this situation. Plan carefully a win-win strategy for resolving this issue. Problem solving from a collaborative position is, more often than not, the best possible choice.

5. **Execute your planned strategy.**

6. **Evaluate your effectiveness.**
   Revisit the results, your plan, your ability to stay with the plan, any secondary problems that may have been created, and what you will do differently the next time.

Orientation and Training

The purpose of training is to facilitate performance.

Robert F. Mager
What Every Manager Should Know About Training

Orientation and Training

Most executives, when asked, will say that people are their most important resource. Yet, once new employees are recruited and hired, the orientation and training they receive often doesn't reflect that sentiment.

Well planned orientation and training can reduce turnover and help ensure a return on the investment made in bringing new employees on board. Whether an organization has two employees or 20,000, it needs to help its employees succeed.

As a coach in your organization, you have the responsibility for orienting and training your individual employees so they become an integral part of your team.

Orientation is the process of acquainting employees with the organization and people with whom they will work. The more comfortable new employees are with their surroundings and their new coworkers, the sooner they will be productive.

Orientation is not just something you do on the first day and consists of much more than just having them read the policy and procedure manual. Orientation is ongoing and may take anywhere from two weeks to six months depending on the employee and the complexity of the job.

Once you understand the benefits of a planned orientation and begin to use an orientation checklist, you will find that new employees get in tune with you and your organization much sooner than before.

The four-step training method, which you will learn, can be used to train employees to develop their skills in any type of job. This method is easy to use, and you don't have to be a training expert to use it.

One of the best things about the four-step method is its universal application. Regardless of whether you are in an office, retail, manufacturing, or service industry, the four-step method will work for you.

Your employees' success and, in turn, your success as a coach will be even greater when you use the four-step training method to teach them the skills they need to meet the challenges and requirements of their job.

Orientation Benefits

The five benefits of planned orientation:

1. _____

2. _____

3. _____

4. _____

5. _____

Turning benefits into reality:

1. _____
   _____
   _____

2. _____
   _____
   _____

3. _____
   _____
   _____

4. _____
   _____
   _____

5. _____
   _____
   _____

Four-Step Training Method

1. Preparation

- Define objectives
- Organize materials/equipment
- Arrange the place
- Inform the employee

2. Presentation/Demonstration

- Show and tell steps—Your outline of the learning sequence

3. Tryout

- Have trainee explain the task
- Correct mistakes in a positive manner
- Give feedback on progress
- Be patient
- Back away and let trainee practice alone

4. Follow-Up

- Who should trainee go to?
- Decide how often to check back
- Ask trainee for questions
- Evaluate training results

Developing a Training Plan

1. Preparation

After training, the trainee will be able to:

_____

_____

Materials/Equipment:

_____

_____

Prepare employee and place by:

_____

_____

2. Presentation/Demonstration (Show and Tell)

_____

_____

_____

_____

_____

_____

_____

_____

_____

_____

_____

3. Tryout

During tryout I will have the trainee:

_____

_____

_____

_____

4. Follow-Up

During follow-up I will have the trainee:

_____

_____

_____

_____

_____

_____

_____

_____

Qualities of an Effective Trainer

You don't have to be a training expert to use the four-step training method. Having the qualities below, however, can help you be a successful trainer.

Good Communication Skills
>Use clear and concise language
>Listen as well as speak
>Make frequent eye contact

Knowledge of the Subject
>You don't have to be the best worker, but
>You do need a comprehensive understanding of the subject

Experience
>You should have done the job yourself
>Previous training experience can also be helpful

Patience
>New people will make mistakes
>It may take several attempts before they get it right

Interest in Training
>You have to like to help people
>You feel good when you see people learn
>You take pride in others' successes

Respect for Others
>People view you as knowledgeable
>People see you as trustful

Sense of Humor
>Don't tell jokes, but
>See the humor in the situation

Setting Goals

The secret of success is constancy to purpose.

Benjamin Disraeli

Setting Goals

Most experts agree on the importance of setting goals. Goals provide a sense of direction and purpose. They reveal true priorities. Through them, necessary resources are identified. And, of course, they are one of the most useful tools available for career development.

The most effective goals are specific and measurable. They should clearly state what the expected outcome is, as well as when it is to be achieved. Less specific goals are often called "objectives"—statements of a general aim. Usually, objectives are long-range goals and are supported by shorter-term, more specific goals. Short-term goals are then turned into real accomplishments by daily, supporting activities. This is why so many management and personal development experts stress the importance of a daily or weekly "to-do" list. Regular, daily work is what makes "goals" become "reality."

Tips for the daily list...

Make it as simple or complex as you want. Just make it comfortable and workable for you.

Make sure goals are included by breaking them down into small, manageable activities.

Your "to-do" list should reflect your typical schedule. If two-thirds of your day is spent responding to unexpected requests, don't try to plan items for more than one-third of your day.

Prioritize your tasks and be sure to spend either most of your time or your best quality time on the most important items.

Goals are useful not only in career development but in personal development as well. Aims such as losing weight, learning another language, starting a new hobby, or saving money become reality much more often when they are turned into goal statements that are supported by daily activities.

The role a coach or mentor plays in helping a protégé establish directions and set goals cannot be understated. Indeed, it could easily become the single most important contribution we make to someone's professional life. At the same time, we should take care to guide our protégés so that their goals are realistic (goals should be challenging, but not unattainable). Bitter personal disappointment can result when care is not taken in the goal-setting process. To help others avoid disappointment, we should

- help ensure that long-range goals are balanced with short-range goals, and difficult goals are broken into smaller, manageable pieces
- remind them that goals are for them, not others. They should choose goals that are important to them or are enjoyable.
- help them find value in their effort even when they fall short of their goal
- remind them that their goals should build on the talents and skills they already have, which are a precious resource

---

A Goal-Setting Quiz

Answer each item True or False.

_____ 1. Really effective goals are not measurable.

_____ 2. Goals are usually most effective if they are beyond reach.

_____ 3. The more goals, the better.

_____ 4. Goals should be compatible with each other.

_____ 5. Goals should have a time frame or deadline associated with them.

Answers on following page.

Answers to *A Goal-Setting Quiz*

1. **False**. Some goals (such as satisfaction) are indeed hard to measure, but there are generally ways to do so. Try asking, "How will I know when it happens?" or, "How do I know when it's not happening?" The answer will usually reveal how to measure the goal.

2. **False**. Unattainable goals are a source of frustration and discouragement. Goals should be challenging but not hopeless.

3. **False**. Too many goals spread resources and attention too thinly. Most experts agree on a general range of three to seven as ideal.

4. **True**. Otherwise, for example, you may have a goal to "buy a new boat" at the same time as a goal to "save money for a new home."

5. **True**. A time frame is what makes a "wish" become a "goal."

Setting Career Goals
Worksheet

Vision

_____
_____
_____

↑

Long-Range
Goals

_____
_____
_____
_____

↑

Short-Range
Goals

_____
_____
_____
_____

↑

Supporting
Activities

_____
_____
_____
_____

Setting Career Goals
Worksheet

Vision

⬆

Long-Range Goals

⬆

Short-Range Goals

⬆

Supporting Activities

_____

_____

_____

_____

_____

_____

_____

_____

_____

_____

_____

_____

_____

_____

_____

_____

_____

_____

_____

_____

Suggested Process for
Protégé Goal Setting

Meeting One: *The importance of career goals; the four-
step goal setting process.*

Meeting Two: *The protégé's career vision; long-range
goals.*

Meeting Three: *The protégé's goals; support activities.*

Meeting Four: *Progress check.*

Delegation

Proper delegation is an indication of a manager's trust and faith in his people.

James F. Evered

Delegation

Delegation is the ability to reassign your work responsibilities to your employees so that your time is saved and they experience professional development. Delegation is transferring a portion of your responsibility and decision-making authority to someone who works for you. Delegation can and does build people, in addition to strengthening relationships, communication, and trust. The leadership style that uses delegation to build the team also prepares the department to weather change more effectively.

On the other hand, the lack of delegation is clearly apparent in poor morale, tedium, lack of trust, and an overall hopeless/helpless attitude on the part of everyone that says, *I've more to do than time to do it.* Yet, even when the symptoms are clear, we are often slow to respond.

Why are we so hesitant to delegate? Even with numerous benefits so obvious and acknowledged, the rationalizations for *not* delegating are legion. We can always justify our reluctance to trust, to train, to grant authority and decision making with dozens of excuses. Some of those reasons are valid. Some of them radiate from the person we are. Some of them simply hold us back from actualizing ourselves and the people who trust us with their careers. We need to be able to know not only *how* to delegate but *when* to give the work away and to whom. True, there are some jobs that cannot be delegated. Yet there are far more bogey men perceived to be in the closet than truly exist. We must come to grips with our fears about delegating and practice this skill until it becomes second nature, until it is a leadership habit.

Jethro, Moses' father-in-law, saw the need and intervened with words of advice that still ring clear today: *"...the work is too heavy for you; you cannot handle it alone...teach them...show them...appoint them...if you do this...you will be able to stand the strain and all the people will go home satisfied." (Exodus 18:17-23)* Even in our modern high-tech environment, the effective management skill of delegation is as appropriate today as it was centuries ago. Delegation is essential for the manager who wants to *be able to stand the strain and send the people home satisfied.*

We talk a lot these days about empowerment and how we should or could empower, and yet we fail to recognize that empowerment for teams, or for individuals, is built on the foundation of capable delegation.

Managers who wish to increase production, develop competent employees, provide the company with people who have promotion potential, and create an atmosphere that fosters morale should look again at delegation. Work through these next few pages with the resolution that you will tap the incredible resource of your people-power with this art, this science, called delegation.

Delegation Self-Assessment

As a manager of people,	Yes	No
I had/have a role model that demonstrated above-average delegation skills.	____	____
I have a great deal of trust in my employees.	____	____
I am good at planning and organizing the work that needs to be done.	____	____
I can effectively determine what type of jobs and assignments would challenge and motivate my people.	____	____
I am willing to take the time to train those who would benefit in order for them to succeed.	____	____
I am fully aware that if my people succeed in their assignments I will be perceived as an effective manager.	____	____
I am confident in my relationship with my management.	____	____
I select the jobs I will give to my subordinates based on what I know about them, their skills, and their interests.	____	____
I understand quite well that I cannot do all that is required by myself and am more than willing to delegate to meet production and service needs.	____	____
I am aware that most of my people could experience greater professional development with the more frequent use of my delegation skills.	____	____
Total	____	____

More *Yes* responses than *No*'s would indicate a better understanding of and perhaps more use of the delegation ability in supervision responsibilities. An unusually high number of *No* responses would signal a need to practice delegation more often.

Do's and Don'ts of Delegation

Step #1

_____

_____

Step #2

_____

_____

Step #3

_____

_____

Step #4 _____

a. _____

b. _____

c. _____

d. _____

e. _____

f. _____

Step #5

_____

_____

Who to Do What When

Who (Employee)	**What** (Task)	**When** (Date assigned)
1. _____	_____	_____
2. _____	_____	_____
3. _____	_____	_____
4. _____	_____	_____
5. _____	_____	_____
6. _____	_____	_____
7. _____	_____	_____
8. _____	_____	_____
9. _____	_____	_____
10. _____	_____	_____
11. _____	_____	_____
12. _____	_____	_____
13. _____	_____	_____
14. _____	_____	_____
15. _____	_____	_____

Enabling Employees to Succeed

There are no problems we cannot solve together, and very few that we can solve by ourselves.

Lyndon Baines Johnson

Enabling Employees to Succeed

Coaches wear many "hats." They counsel, help set direction, and give feedback. They make assignments that develop skills. And, they help to make success possible. They do this by anticipating problems and obstacles their protégé will face and by providing the resources their protégé will need. On one hand, they help the protégé avoid failure; on the other hand, they help the protégé achieve success. By removing obstacles and providing resources, good coaches are "enablers" for their protégés.

Think of someone learning a new skill, such as playing golf. If you play golf, you might remember the roadblocks you faced in learning the game. If you were lucky, someone provided some key resources.

Learning the Game of Golf

Roadblocks

Fear
Ignorance of proper grip or stance
Poor clubs (or no clubs!)
Bad habits

Resources

Opportunity to practice
Lessons
Good equipment
Patience

Think of a new skill or assignment in your own life. Can you recall the roadblocks you faced? The resources (perhaps as simple as good advice) someone provided?

Task: _____

Roadblocks: _____

_____

_____

_____

Resources: _____

_____

_____

_____

Enabling Employees to Succeed

What is enabling?

1. Removing _____ that will prevent success.

   Examples:

2. Providing _____ that will help ensure success.

   Examples:

The Videotape Project

McClelland Systems, Incorporated, located in Chicago, Illinois, is a manufacturer of precision gauges and measuring instruments. McClelland has a distributor network of 25 company stores that distribute the company's products.

Terry Hulsey, Vice President of Human Resources with McClelland, recently won a long and hard-fought battle to initiate a flexible benefits program for McClelland's employees. This new flexible benefits program will permit employees to select from a variety of benefits. These will include health insurance, catastrophic medical insurance, life insurance, dental insurance, and vision care, as well as the opportunity to purchase extra time for holidays and vacations. Options will also include a flexible spending account to allow employees a chance to set aside pre-tax dollars for day care, elder care, or reimbursement of their medical deductible.

This program was resisted by McClelland's senior management because of the increased administrative burden it will create and the difficulty of coordinating flexible benefits in McClelland's many stores.

Hulsey has selected Chris Snodgrass to produce a key element of the communication campaign to announce the program and explain how the benefits work. Snodgrass is a young employee who has been with McClelland for 18 months working as an administrative assistant in the Compensation and Benefits Department of Human Resources. Chris's assignment is to produce a videotape for distribution to all facilities that will communicate the value of this new program and provide details in converting coverage from the old program to the new, making changes throughout the benefit year, making claims when necessary, and other details.

Snodgrass has limited experience in videotape production. Chris was involved as a narrator on a previous videotape which was produced by the in-house video department. Chris has also written one or two scripts, but has never supervised full production of a videotape. This may be a problem because two members of the in-house video technical staff were laid off in a recent cost-cutting attempt, leaving the video production department at only one-half its former level. Employees in the video production department have traditionally resented and resisted efforts by "outsiders" to be actively involved in the production process. The video production department reports to the Administrative Services Division, headed by Pat Wilson, a colleague of Hulsey.

The new videotape is to be produced within 60 days. Distribution will be to all 25 distributors in the continental United States. All but two of these distributors are on identical benefit packages. Two, however, have slight differences because of company/union-negotiated agreements that prescribe certain death benefit limits and medical insurance coverage.

This videotape is an unplanned project. Budget money for this project will have to be diverted from other Human Resource priorities. Chris Snodgrass's first task, therefore, will be to recommend what other Human Resource projects will need to be canceled or delayed in order to fund this project. Chris will have to discuss this with Dale DiSanto, who is Manager of the Employee Relations Department and serves as the coordinator of the Human Resources department budget activities.

A new employee has recently joined the Communication Division. This employee, Kelly Allison, was recently a weekend broadcaster with Channel 7 News. Hulsey has a vague recollection of Channel 7 being involved in the production of a videotape at a recent insurance benefits conference held in the Chicago area. That videotape "seemed" to follow a general model that would be useful in this new project.

Discussion Questions:

1. What roadblocks will cause problems for Chris Snodgrass?

2. What resources might Terry Hulsey consider lining up that would aid Chris with this project?

3. How closely should Hulsey supervise Snodgrass during this project?

4. Assume you are in Chris's position. Develop an action plan to complete the project.

Enabling My Employees

Instructions: List employees who report to you, and one or two of each employee's major tasks or functions. For each task, identify at least one actual or potential roadblock and at least one resource needed for the employee to be successful in the task. Finally, set a target date to take action on the roadblocks/resources listed.

Employee	Task or Function	Roadblock	Resources Needed	Date

Observing and Measuring Performance

Simple, visible measures of what's important should mark every square foot of every department of every operation.

Tom Peters
Thriving on Chaos

Observing and Measuring Performance

Successful athletic coaches watch game films to observe and measure the performance of their players. They may watch the same game several times just to spot the things that their players are doing well and where they need to improve.

The knowledge the coach gains watching films is then used during the next practice session to help the players improve their performance. Coaches are able to work on specific techniques and skills that can help their team win the next game.

Coaches in the business world don't have the luxury of watching films of their employees at work. Frequently they even miss seeing the real "play" of their employees. They may get an "instant replay" later, but it's likely to be tinted by the view of the person providing the replay.

Effective coaches in the business world use systems to observe and measure employee performance. These managers then use the performance information to provide feedback to their employees.

Successful managers take time to observe employee performance. When observing performance, these managers look at both the end results and the process. For example, when you order a meal at a restaurant, you see the end result when the plate is set in front of you. It may look good, but taste terrible. To find the source of the bad taste (end result), you would need to observe the steps (process) used in preparing your meal.

It's difficult to know how well your people are doing without observing their work. And, if you don't know how well your people are doing, it's hard to fulfill one of your primary roles as a coach—helping employees improve their performance.

Observing performance needs to be done on a regular, recurring basis. Learning how to observe without making employees feel threatened or intimidated is a necessary coaching skill that you'll learn in this session.

Successful managers also use tracking systems to measure performance over time. They know if today's results are better, worse, or the same as yesterday's results. They frequently use graphs to track performance and compare the actual results with previously established goals.

During this session you'll learn how to develop and use various methods and systems to improve your ability to observe and measure performance.

Observing and Measuring Performance

Why observing and measuring performance is important:

Two things to look at when observing are:

-

-

Sample Observation Checklist of
Basic Word Processing Functions

_____ Opening a new document
_____ Saving a document
_____ Deleting a document
_____ Typing and revising
_____ Printing
_____ Using help and on-line lessons
_____ Character formatting
_____ Paragraph formatting
_____ Using style sheets
_____ Setting margins
_____ Formatting
_____ Spell check
_____ Glossaries

My Observation Checklist for _____

_____ _____
_____ _____
_____ _____
_____ _____
_____ _____
_____ _____
_____ _____
_____ _____
_____ _____
_____ _____
_____ _____
_____ _____

How to Observe

- Observe process used

- Observe end result

- Explain why you are observing

- Don't interrupt work flow

- Ask questions to verify your understanding

- Watch operation several times

- Make notes for discussion

- Compare observations with any written procedures

- Observe other employees for comparison purposes

- Be aware of your influence on the employee's performance

Things to remember when developing tracking systems:

Alternative methods of tracking performance:

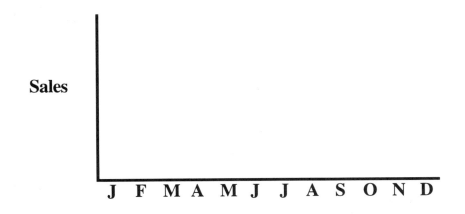

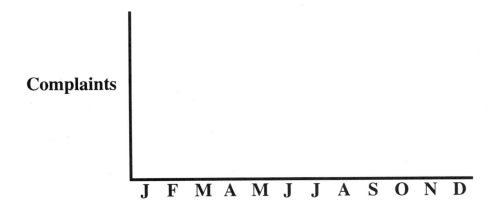

Performance graphs I can use and their axes:

Performance	Goal	Time
_____	_____	_____
_____	_____	_____
_____	_____	_____
_____	_____	_____
_____	_____	_____
_____	_____	_____
_____	_____	_____
_____	_____	_____

Things I want to remember about analyzing results:

Things I want to remember about giving feedback:

Unconventional Measures

In his book *Thriving on Chaos* (Alfred A. Knopf, Inc., 1987), management consultant Tom Peters suggests several unconventional ways to measure performance. Included in his list are:

Prescription	Measure
Niche Creation	Number of "differentiators" added to each product every 90 days
Service	The ten attributes of customer satisfactions; customer evaluation of the intangibles; the lifetime value of a customer
Listening	Informal listening ("call three customers per week")
Pilots	Number of pilot tests of anything going on in each area
Teams	Percentage of people in team configurations
Recognition	Number of recognition acts/events per month
Training	Hours/dollars devoted to skill upgrading
Management by Example	Time spent per day/week on top priority

Feedback

Help people reach their full potential. Catch them doing something right.

Ken Blanchard and Spencer Johnson
The One Minute Manager

Feedback

Effective coaches provide regular feedback to their employees about their performance. Ken Blanchard and Spencer Johnson, authors of *The One Minute Manager,* say that feedback is the "breakfast of champions."

Most people want and need feedback about their job performance. It has been estimated that 80 percent of the performance problems that occur in the workplace could be solved with better use of feedback.

Feedback can be either positive or corrective, depending on the situation. Unfortunately, many managers give more corrective feedback than positive feedback even though their people do things right more often than they make mistakes.

Positive feedback is an effective management tool. Research has shown that "recognition strengthens performance"—when you tell employees they do a good job, they are more likely to do a good job again in the future. People will work hard and long and go to extraordinary lengths if they know what they do is recognized and appreciated.

Corrective feedback is used to help employees improve their performance. Bringing performance problems to the attention of employees is part of the job of a manager. When giving corrective feedback, the manager's goal should be to eliminate the negative behavior and keep the employee.

Some managers have different perceptions than their employees about the frequency, type, and quality of feedback they give to their employees. The feedback instrument provided in this workbook will help you evaluate the feedback you provide to your employees and identify areas where your feedback might be improved.

In this session you'll learn about the 80/20 rule when giving feedback and also have the opportunity to give and receive both positive and corrective feedback. Increasing the frequency and effectiveness of your feedback can make you a better coach and lead to better employee performance.

Feedback Evaluation—Self

Read each statement below and circle the number that you think best describes the feedback you give your employees.

I think that I...

		Rarely	Sometimes	Often
1.	Provide positive feedback	1 2	3 4 5	6 7
2.	Provide specific feedback	1 2	3 4 5	6 7
3.	Provide sincere feedback	1 2	3 4 5	6 7
4.	Give corrective feedback	1 2	3 4 5	6 7
5.	Criticize behavior not the person	1 2	3 4 5	6 7
6.	Provide help to improve	1 2	3 4 5	6 7
7.	Try to find the good in things rather than the bad	1 2	3 4 5	6 7
8.	Focus on what's right	1 2	3 4 5	6 7
9.	Listen to employees	1 2	3 4 5	6 7
10.	Use graphs, charts, etc. to provide feedback	1 2	3 4 5	6 7
11.	Offer support to employees	1 2	3 4 5	6 7
12.	Pass on positive feedback received from others	1 2	3 4 5	6 7
13.	Praise more than criticize	1 2	3 4 5	6 7

Total Score: _____

Feedback Evaluation—Employees

Read each statement below and circle the number that you think best describes the feedback you receive from your supervisor.

I think that my supervisor…

		Rarely	Sometimes	Often
1.	Provides positive feedback	1 2	3 4 5	6 7
2.	Provides specific feedback	1 2	3 4 5	6 7
3.	Provides sincere feedback	1 2	3 4 5	6 7
4.	Gives corrective feedback	1 2	3 4 5	6 7
5.	Criticizes behavior not the person	1 2	3 4 5	6 7
6.	Provides help to improve	1 2	3 4 5	6 7
7.	Tries to find the good in things rather than the bad	1 2	3 4 5	6 7
8.	Focuses on what's right	1 2	3 4 5	6 7
9.	Listens to employees	1 2	3 4 5	6 7
10.	Uses graphs, charts, etc. to provide feedback	1 2	3 4 5	6 7
11.	Offers support to employees	1 2	3 4 5	6 7
12.	Passes on positive feedback received from others	1 2	3 4 5	6 7
13.	Praises more than criticizes	1 2	3 4 5	6 7

Total Score: _____

Giving Positive Feedback

Key Point: *Recognition Strengthens Performance*

B = Behavior

E = Effect

T = Thank You

Positive Feedback Action Plan

Employee   Action that requires positive feedback

_____   _____

_____   _____

_____   _____

_____   _____

_____   _____

_____   _____

_____   _____

_____   _____

Giving Corrective Feedback

Goal: *Eliminate behavior, keep the employee*

B = Behavior

E = Effect

E = Expectation

R = Result

Corrective Feedback Action Plan

Employee   Action that requires corrective feedback

_____   _____

_____   _____

_____   _____

_____   _____

_____   _____

_____   _____

_____   _____

When Giving Feedback . . .

The following basic principles apply whether you are giving employees positive or corrective feedback. Keep these principles in mind the next time you give feedback.

Specific

Don't just say "good job" or "that's not right." Be specific about the behavior you want repeated or eliminated. Tell the employee what you liked and you are more likely to see that behavior again. Don't beat around the bush when providing corrective feedback, let the employee know specifically what was wrong.

Immediate

Tell the employee as soon as possible. The closer the feedback to the performance, the more impact it will have. Don't wait for two or three days to give feedback. Do it now!

Earned

False praise can have a negative effect on employees who know they don't deserve it. It can also cause resentment among other employees who think you can't tell the difference between good and bad performance. When giving corrective feedback, be sure you have your facts straight and that you're talking to the employee who "earned" the corrective feedback.

Individualized

Use the person's name so he/she knows the feedback is directed to him/her. The personal touch is especially important when giving positive feedback because people like to hear their names when you are saying something good about their work.

The Coaching Model

Coaching: A directive process by a manager to train and orient an employee to the realities of the workplace and to help the employee remove barriers to optimum work performance.

Marianne Minor
Coaching and Counseling

The Coaching Model

When the performance of an employee does not meet expectations, or developmental goals are missed because of performance deficiencies, effective coaches know that it is their responsibility to help their people get back on track.

Some typical problems that may require intervention are when a person's performance, which has been good, begins to slip; a person is having trouble meeting commitments; a person obviously needs help in resolving a problem; or a person comes to you and asks for assistance.

Whenever you need to address any of these or similar situations, the following coaching model can be used:

1. Get agreement that a problem exists.
2. Decide on a solution.
3. Follow up.
4. Give recognition when the problem is solved.

Getting agreement that a problem exists can often be the most time consuming and most difficult step in the process. However, without the employee's "buy-in" that a problem exists, the other steps are not likely to result in any long-term performance improvement.

Deciding on a solution also requires employee buy-in. In fact, the best results are normally obtained when the employee is the one who comes up with the solution. It's always easier for a person to make his/her solution a reality than to do something suggested by someone else.

Following up is the responsibility of the manager and requires a commitment to checking back to see whether or not the employee implemented the solution in a timely manner.

Giving recognition when the problem is solved lets the employee know that you noticed and appreciated their efforts to improve the situation. Failure to provide recognition can result in the employee reverting back to the original problem.

Each step of the process is important and must be followed if the intervention is to be successful. The coaching model requires the use of two-way communication. In fact, the employee should be doing most of the talking and the coach most of the listening.

The model is also most effective when the manager has the ability to use numerous other coaching skills such as goal setting, observing and measuring performance, building trust, and giving feedback.

Coaching Model

When the performance of their people does not meet expectations, or developmental goals are missed because of performance deficiencies, effective coaches use a four-step process to solve performance problems.

Get Agreement that a Problem Exists

- Ask questions to see if the person is aware of the problem
- Ensure that the person understands the consequences of the problem
- Get agreement from the person that a problem exists

Decide on a Solution

- Ask questions to involve the person with the problem
- Generate as many alternatives to the problem as possible
- Help the person think through the problem
- Let the person think through the problem
- Agree on the solution(s) that will be implemented
- Agree on a timetable for implementing the solution(s)

Follow Up

- Check to see whether the solution is implemented
- Determine whether the solution is implemented on schedule
- Determine whether the solution is working

Give Recognition When the Problem Is Solved

- Give specific feedback
- Be sincere when you give feedback
- Remember that "recognition strengthens performance"

Coaching Worksheet

Use this worksheet to think about a current performance problem you have with one of your people and to develop a plan for resolving the problem. Refer to it during the discussion to help keep yourself on track.

Employee: _____

Date of planned discussion: _____

Describe the problem that you think exists.

_____

_____

Step 1: *Get Agreement that a Problem Exists*

What questions will you ask?

What did you agree to as the problem?

Step 2: *Decide on a Solution*

What are the alternatives?

What solution(s) did you agree to implement? By when?

Step 3: *Follow Up*

When will you follow up?

How will you know the solution is working?

Step 4: *Give Recognition When the Problem Is Solved*

What type of recognition will you give?

What will you do to help keep the problem from happening again?

Motivation and Morale

Human motivation rests on one fundamental principal: All people (peak performers and all others as well) are motivated, at bottom, by self-interest. It's what is called the WIIFM principle—"What's in it for me?"

Gerald Kushel
Reaching the Peak Performance Zone

Motivation and Morale

All behavior is motivated, but the motivation is different for each person. The coach's job is to create an environment where people can motivate themselves. Providing such an environment requires understanding the major motivational theories and being able to apply them to the workplace.

The motivation theories you will learn about in this session include Maslow's Hierarchy of Needs, Herzberg's Two Factor Theory, McGregor's Theory X-Y, and B.F. Skinner's theory of rewards and punishment. Each theory provides insights into why people do what they do and can help you understand differences in individual employee behavior.

Morale depends on job satisfaction and job satisfaction is achieved by meeting people's individual needs. However, there are some things you can do to improve the morale for your whole work team.

Effective coaches know that to keep morale up it's important to *keep communication open and free* to reduce or eliminate rumors. They also know they must *maintain a positive attitude* because it will rub off on those around them.

High morale also requires a coach who can *listen and encourage feedback* from employees. Successful coaches *help employees achieve their goals.* People who know you are interested in them and want to help them are going to be more likely to have a positive attitude and better morale.

Providing rewards and recognition to employees when they meet established goals and expectations is another way effective coaches motivate their employees and maintain high morale. During this session you'll brainstorm several different types of rewards that you can provide to employees to reinforce their positive contributions.

As a manager you need to invest time getting to know your people. Try to find out what motivates them and what they expect out of their jobs and out of you. The more you know about your people, the better you will be able to do what it takes to create an environment where your people are motivated to do their best.

Maslow's Hierarchy of Needs

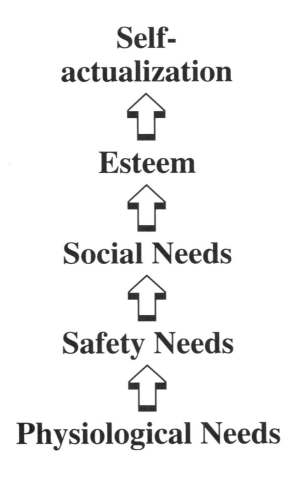

Self-actualization

⬆

Esteem

⬆

Social Needs

⬆

Safety Needs

⬆

Physiological Needs

What Maslow's Theory means to me is

_____ _____

_____ _____

_____ _____

Herzberg's Two Factor Theory

- Hygiene Factors
  - ◆ Comfort and security

- Satisfiers
  - ◆ Personal growth and development

What Herzberg's Theory means to me is

_____ _____

_____ _____

_____ _____

McGregor's Theory X-Y

- X = lazy, avoid work and responsibility

- Y = seek responsibility and involvement

What McGregor's Theory means to me is

_____ _____

_____ _____

_____ _____

B. F. Skinner

- Rewarded behavior
  - ♦ Tends to be repeated

- Punishment
  - ♦ Discourages unacceptable behavior

- Neutral (ignoring behavior)
  - ♦ Indicates the behavior doesn't matter

What Skinner's Theory means to me is

_____   _____

_____   _____

_____   _____

Motivation Worksheet

Directions:

(1) Write your employees' names in the left-hand column.
(2) List one or more specific actions you will take to create a motivational environment.

Employee	Action Required

Improving Morale

1. Keep communication open and free.

2. Maintain a positive attitude yourself.

3. Listen and encourage feedback.

4. Help employees achieve their goals.

Specific things that I can do to improve the morale of my employees:

_____   _____

_____   _____

_____   _____

_____   _____

_____   _____

_____   _____

_____   _____

_____   _____

_____   _____

_____   _____

Recognition and Reward Ideas

Free

_____

_____

_____

_____

$10 or less

_____

_____

_____

_____

$11 - $25

_____

_____

_____

_____

Over $25

_____

_____

_____

_____

Types of Employees

Men and women want to do a good job, and if they are provided the proper environment, they will do so.

Bill Hewlett, founder, Hewlett-Packard

Types of Employees

Flexibility! Skill, attitude, or talent? Regardless, that characteristic is key for the effective coach/leader. Being both willing and able to adapt to the demands of the situation and the people makes the difference between success and failure in today's workplace. One size no longer fits all. Just because *"I said so and I'm the boss,"* worked in the past, there are no guarantees it will bring positive results in the new work environment.

Employees come in many different shapes and sizes. (And this is not a section on diversity.) This portion of the study deals with the stages of growth a person experiences as they learn and work at their job. Each of us can think back and remember ourselves as the new employee. We can feel the excitement; excitement mixed with anxiety as it dawned on us how ill-prepared we were to start this new job.

The new employee needs a different type of supervision style from the one they will need when they have been fully trained. A less directive approach will be even more appropriate when that employee has matured to a self-directed, highly-motivated, work-experienced team member.

Those different leadership styles flow out of one flexible manager, not two or three or four. The effective leader of today is able to analyze the demands of a situation, the growth needs of the employee and provide the right style at the right time. That requires the ability and willingness to be flexible. Today's manager will break under the changing work environment and employee requirements if they are not able to bend.

This section of the workbook provides insight into people. To be an effective coach and mentor, we must first be students of human nature. From there you will be guided through suitable responses for the circumstance. Each of us reacts naturally in a certain way. That style, or way, is one we have either learned or one that is a tendency for us. While natural and comfortable for us, those tendency reactions are not always the best choice. To choose to respond, rather than to react, in a way that is neither comfortable nor natural but right is to be an effective, flexible coach.

Employee Growth Stages

New Employee	Trainee	Skilled Worker	High Performer
• *Very enthusiastic* • *In need of training and orientation*	• *Becoming skilled* • *Frustrated with inability to be more involved*	• *Very capable* • *Attitude varies* • *Can be a problem employee*	• *Competent and Committed*

Notes:

_____

_____

_____

_____

_____

_____

_____

_____

Leadership Style Survey

There are four generally accepted styles of leadership. These styles are reflected in the questions that follow. Think about your leadership skill and recent situations as you answer the questions. Use the following scale to respond to each question.

4—Always   3—Usually   2—Sometimes   1—Never

When using my leadership style, I tend to ...

_____ 1. Provide specific, detailed directions.

_____ 2. Explain decisions, solicit ideas.

_____ 3. Ask employees to define how to do the task.

_____ 4. Allow employees to develop an action plan.

_____ 5. Develop action plans to solve problems.

_____ 6. Make final decisions after hearing employees' ideas.

_____ 7. Listen/facilitate employees' problem solving.

_____ 8. Allow employees to solve problems without advice.

(Adapted from an exercise in 50 Activities for Coaching/Mentoring, *by Donna Berry, Charles Cadwell, and Joe Fehrmann, HRD Press, Amherst, Mass., 1993.)*

Leadership Styles

Director	Coach	Supporter	Delegator
Supervises closely	*Coaches*	*Coaches*	*Hands-off*
Trains	*Trains*	*Encourages*	*mentor style*
One-way	*More*	*Two-way*	*Lets worker*
communicator	*supportive*	*communicator*	*alone*
	Two-way		*Listens*
	communicator		

1. _____   2. _____   3. _____   4. _____
5. _____   6. _____   7. _____   8. _____
Total _____   Total _____   Total _____   Total _____

Totals for your answers will indicate style.

Notes:

_____

_____

_____

_____

_____

_____

_____

_____

Employees' Needs for Leadership

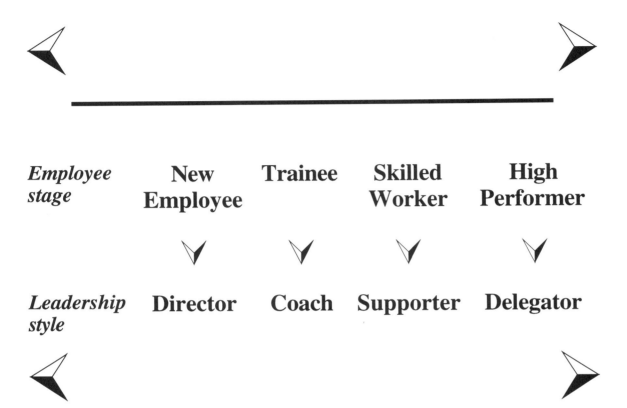

Employee stage	New Employee	Trainee	Skilled Worker	High Performer
Leadership style	Director	Coach	Supporter	Delegator

Name That Employee's Leadership Needs

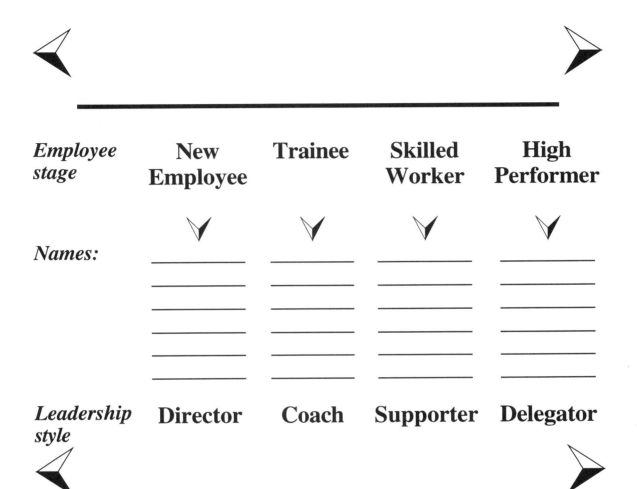

Employee stage	New Employee	Trainee	Skilled Worker	High Performer
Names:	_____ _____ _____ _____ _____ _____	_____ _____ _____ _____ _____ _____	_____ _____ _____ _____ _____ _____	_____ _____ _____ _____ _____ _____
Leadership style	Director	Coach	Supporter	Delegator

Role of the Mentor

Mentors have an important impact on organizations…The mentor-protégé relationship is an association of two individuals in which the person of greater rank or expertise teaches, counsels, guides and helps the other develop both personally and professionally. The **Dictionary of Occupational Titles** *ranks it as the highest and most complex level of functioning in the people-related hierarchy of skills.*

Elizabeth Alleman
*Manual: Alleman Leadership
Development Questionnaire*

Role of the Mentor

Since man began to record his life on the walls of caves, mentoring has been journalized as a way of developing the younger, less experienced person. In some cases, mentoring is the practice of apprenticeship. In other, more common situations, mentoring is the art of caring for another person. Mentoring includes support, encouragement, guidance, communicating vision and promise, and investing time above and beyond what would normally be expected.

Mentoring has become a more accepted term for planned professional development in the workplace during the past decade. Management has begun to see the advantages of matching the experienced to the less experienced; the older to the younger; the wise to the uninitiated. In some cases, such as Pizza Hut World Offices, the practice is formal and guaranteed standardized by a mentoring procedure. In other organizations, the process is informal and evolves naturally when two people recognize a kindred spirit and the long-term employee chooses to "sponsor" the newer person. Whatever the means, the result is the same: workers feel valued and more often reach their professional possibility.

More than likely, each of us has gained from a similar relationship in our own lives. For some it has been a relative to whom we felt especially close. For others it was a teacher, a coach, a neighbor, a supervisor, or even a coworker. Whomever that person was, he or she gave us good advice, was there to listen, to comfort, to direct, and to help us to see promise, create goals, and find direction. This person often believed in our potential when we found that difficult to do.

This part of the study looks at mentoring as slightly different from coaching but nonetheless important to the growth of the people who work for us. As you consider the worth of this practice you will begin to conceive of the many ways you can use a mentoring approach to improve people and the environment.

I caution you to rethink the section that addressed different employee types. Not all of us relate to each and everyone we work with. For that matter, not to everyone we *live* with. Most of the time you will be wise to link people who are similar to one another. There is a greater likelihood for trust and understanding in those relationships and therefore more chance of success for your mentoring program.

Odysseus, king of Ithaca, gave us the meaning for "mentor." When he had to leave to fight in the Trojan War, he turned over his son and his household to Mentor. Serving as teacher and overseer, this trusted guide offered care, advice, friendship, and training. Mentoring is a practice that can help move working America toward fulfilling its potential.

> *Companies need to encourage people to form relationships and give them the skills to do so. They should create the environment where people will naturally gravitate towards each other.*
>
> Kathleen Kram
> International Management

A Mentor in My Life

"My _____ has been/is a mentor in my life and as a mentor _____ me."

We have defined the role of mentor *as:*

_____

_____

_____

Adding to that definition includes:

_____

_____

_____

Mentoring Debate ...

"A mentoring program in my company would have great value to the organization and the individuals involved."

Why?	*Why Not?*
1.	1.
2.	2.
3.	3.
4.	4.
5.	5.
6.	6.
7.	7.

Building Trust

You may be deceived if you trust too much, but you will live in torment if you don't trust enough.

Frank Crane

Building Trust

Trust is probably the most fragile commodity coaches have. Trust, like respect, is earned over time, but lost in a moment. Without it, we cannot be effective coaches.

How much we are trusted is usually a reflection of how much we trust others. Douglas McGregor's Theory X and Theory Y model is just as relevant today as it was in the early 1960s. According to McGregor, leaders hold assumptions about people that tend to be either trusting or not trusting. Theory X leaders assume employees would rather not work, and therefore must be controlled, punished, and supervised closely. Theory Y leaders believe that employees want to do a good job, seek responsibility, and can be relied on.

Theory X leaders, who don't trust others, will generally behave in ways that discourage others from trusting them in turn. Theory Y leaders, on the other hand, model the kind of trusting behaviors that make up the most productive mentoring relationships.

Our organizations tend to develop similar X-Y characteristics. In some organizations, risk-taking—even failure—is rewarded, employees help set their own priorities or schedules, and information is communicated quickly and honestly to everyone. Other organizations are "X" organizations: information is hoarded, employees are monitored closely, decision making is centralized, and messengers are routinely shot.

What's My Trust Profile?

	I build others' self-esteem	I admit my own mis-takes	I try to see others' points of view	I follow through on commit-ments	I am open with my feelings	I share informa-tion openly —good and bad	I confront others when necessary
Very high							
High							
Moderate							
Low							
Very low							

What's Our Organization's Trust Profile?

	Employees participate in decision making	Information is consistent-ly and open-ly shared with all	Communica-tion goes up as well as down	Promises are kept	Employees are treated consistently	Risk is rewarded
Very high						
High						
Moderate						
Low						
Very low						

Trust Builders

1. Respect _____.

2. Be open with _____.

3. Admit it when you don't know.

4. Share what you believe is the direction of the organization.

5. Avoid _____.

6. Take _____ when necessary.

7. Trust _____.

8. Practice _____ behavior.

9. Focus on _____ rather than _____.

10. Be consistent in the basis of your decision making.

11. Report bad news quickly.

12. Support team members.

13. _____ _____.

14. Respect _____.

15. Build self-esteem in _____ and _____.

Positioning Your Protégé

Have confidence that if you have done a little thing well, you can do a bigger thing well too.

Storey

Positioning Your Protégé

"Being in the right place at the right time" is a lucky accident for some people and a carefully planned event for others. For a mentor, putting a protégé in the right place at the right time means finding an assignment that both meets a development need and provides an opportunity for others to see the protégé in an appropriate setting.

Two sets of questions need to be answered—what experience would build the protégé's skill or expertise without high risk of failure, and what person or persons is the protégé ready to be exposed to?

Does the protégé need development in:
- professional skills? (such as making presentations, facilitating meetings, or interviewing others)
- leadership skills? (such as managing a project or setting strategic goals)
- management skills? (such as preparing a budget, developing a schedule, or reviewing performance)
- personal skills? (such as meeting others, carrying on nontechnical conversations, or social etiquette)
- technical skills? (such as preparing a financial statement, auditing accounts, or revising a manufacturing process)

Then, does the protégé need exposure to:
- others in the department or division? (such as department heads or supervisors)
- top-level leaders? (such as the President or CEO)
- the organization generally? (such as all employees in a division, or selected employees in several divisions)
- the community? (such as educational or civic leaders)

Putting a protégé in the right place at the right time should not be an accident. It should be the result of careful analysis and planning, and will position the protégé for further success.

Tasks—Benefits

List special *projects* or *assignments* that enhance visibility in this column.	List the personal and technical *skills* and the *networking* benefits in this column.
Company-Wide *Example: Narrate a new product videotape to be shown to all employees*	*Example: public speaking, videotape production, script writing; exposure to all levels*
Top-Level *Example: Present the department's status report at the quarterly president's meeting*	*Example: meeting etiquette, poise under pressure, answering financial questions; the president, other officers*
Department/Division *Example: Coordinate the department's annual budget*	*Example: coordination, time management, interviewing; department supervisors*
Community *Example: Represent the company at the annual National Conference banquet*	*Example: social etiquette, diversity; community leaders*

Action Plan

The following Action Plan puts the ideas of this workshop into practical action. It includes meeting with the protégé to set goals and create assignments that provide the protégé visibility with important persons or groups. These assignments showcase the protégé's skills and abilities. The Action Plan also gives the mentor and the protégé an opportunity to identify professional, technical, or personal skills to develop further. Finally, it gives structure by allowing feedback and a target date for plan completion.

The Plan highlights four areas of visibility:

- Company-Wide—projects that provide visibility or experience on a broad, interdepartmental basis.

- Top-Level—projects that provide exposure to high levels of management.

- Department/Division—projects that increase skill within a functional area.

- Community—projects that allow the protégé to go outside the company and gain social, civic, or charitable experience.

Two copies of the Plan are included. Use the first to draft your own ideas of positioning assignments. Then meet with your protégé and use the second to develop an Action Plan jointly.

Action Plan

For _____ (protégé)

Company-Wide
    Project/Assignment: _____
    Personal Skill Enhancement: _____
    Technical Skill Enhancement: _____
    Networking Benefit: _____
    Target Date: _____

Top-Level
    Project/Assignment: _____
    Personal Skill Enhancement: _____
    Technical Skill Enhancement: _____
    Networking Benefit: _____
    Target Date: _____

Department/Division
    Project/Assignment: _____
    Personal Skill Enhancement: _____
    Technical Skill Enhancement: _____
    Networking Benefit: _____
    Target Date: _____

Community
    Project/Assignment: _____
    Personal Skill Enhancement: _____
    Technical Skill Enhancement: _____
    Networking Benefit: _____
    Target Date: _____

Action Plan

For _____ (protégé)

Company-Wide
    Project/Assignment: _ _____
    Personal Skill Enhancement: _____
    Technical Skill Enhancement: _____
    Networking Benefit: _ _____
    Target Date: _____

Top-Level
    Project/Assignment: _ _____
    Personal Skill Enhancement: _____
    Technical Skill Enhancement: _____
    Networking Benefit: _ _____
    Target Date: _____

Department/Division
    Project/Assignment: _ _____
    Personal Skill Enhancement: _____
    Technical Skill Enhancement: _____
    Networking Benefit: _ _____
    Target Date: _____

Community
    Project/Assignment: _ _____
    Personal Skill Enhancement: _____
    Technical Skill Enhancement: _____
    Networking Benefit: _ _____
    Target Date: _____

Notes

Notes

Notes

Notes